QUOTES

The Wit & Wisdom of
Paris Sleuths

Published

February 8, 2021

Book Cover Art

© Roger Kopman

www.KOPMANPHOTOS.com

First Edition 2021

ISBN-13: 979-8706523268

Printed in the United States of America

DEDICATION:

You know who you are.

This collection of quotes from novels written by Peggy Kopman-Owens was published for you because you once said, *"I will always remember my first trip to Paris, as if it were yesterday."*

Moi, aussi.

SIMON PENNINGTON MYSTERIES:

OUT of TIME in PARIS

FOUND & LOST in PARIS

WAITING in PARIS

MRS. DUCHESNEY MYSTERIES SERIES:

A JAZZ CLUB IN PARIS
Mrs. Duchesney's Mystery at Caveau des Trésors

AN ODD BOUQUET FROM PARIS
Mrs. Duchesney's Mystery in the Flower Market

UNDER A PARIS SKY,
Mrs. Duchesney's Mystery on the Rooftops

A BANK IN PARIS,
Mrs. Duchesney's Mystery along the Seine

A LETTER FROM PARIS,
Mrs. Duchesney's Mystery in the Stamp Market

A KEY TO PARIS,
Mrs. Duchesney's Mystery in Parc Montsouris

Francesca's Story - The Interview

Louie's Story - The Interview

The Education of Francine Robinsworth Duchesney,
A SUMMER ABROAD

More from this author:

THE MIST OF MONTMARTRE

PARIS, APARTMENT FOR RENT

LATE PASSENGER, A NonStop Mystery

SEVEN PARIS MYSTERIES SERIES:

NEVER CHANGE, Montmartre

UNDERGROUND, L' autre Métro

TOO RICH FOR RAIN

THE CLUE, L' Indice

GAMAN, The Japanese Art of Patience

THE SEASONS IN THE GARDEN, Les Saisons dans Le Jardin

THE PROMISE, Ypóschesi

Books co-authored with Michael D. Owens:

A SPECIAL TALENT IN A PLACE CALLED HEAVEN

WINDWARD HOME

SEVEN SHORT STORIES FOR STAGE

"My mother, whose shadow appears in the photograph above, wrote stories and songs, becoming my inspiration. She taught that passion and patience are inseparable partners. From my father and mother, both musicians who loved to travel, I learned to embrace a world full of diversity and endless possibilities. I can never thank them enough for bestowing this lovingly unselfish gift of intellectual freedom."

Table of Contents

Le Détective Français
The French Sleuth

"In Paris,
a person couldn't toss a baguette into the bushes
without hitting a private detective."

- UNDER A PARIS SKY

*"In Paris,
everything was fixable for the right price.
Everything."*

– THE CLUE, L' Indice

*"A bank in Paris was not a safe place
to hide a man's secrets."*

- A BANK IN PARIS

"Only those things we fear losing
have any real value."

- FOUND AND LOST IN PARIS

"I needed thieves.
Without them,
I'd be unemployed."

– OUT OF TIME IN PARIS

*"Once a sleuth made his name in Paris,
there was no need to advertise."*

- FOUND AND LOST IN PARIS

"Could not anyone in Paris keep a secret?"

- OUT OF TIME IN PARIS

"Lesson Ten:
Life was meant to be a mystery. "

– PARIS APARTMENT FOR RENT

*"Every sunrise held promise.
Every sunset, a mystery."*
– A KEY TO PARIS

*"Together, they were unstoppable,
dogs to a hunt
when the scent of a mystery was in the air. "*
– A KEY TO PARIS

"Thieves are like tourists.
They enjoy their souvenirs."

– AN ODD BOUQUET FROM PARIS

"One had to think like a thief
in order to catch a thief."

- FOUND AND LOST IN PARIS

*"(He) was far more an artist, than he was a detective. ...
The artist and the detective constantly battled for his soul."*

– A LETTER FROM PARIS

*"I should not expect you to understand.
You are a sleuth, not an artist."*

- FOUND AND LOST IN PARIS

*"I would be rude to embarrass even a thief
in his favorite place to dine."*

- FOUND AND LOST IN PARIS

*"What was life or love
without a bit of competition
and a little mystery?"*

– UNDER A PARIS SKY

"My specialty is art thefts.
I do apologize,
if you have been misled."

- WAITING IN PARIS

"If your dog had been recommended instead,
I would have hired him."

– OUT OF TIME IN PARIS

L' Ami Loyal Français
The Sleuth's Best Friend

*"I am a cat
in a city of dogs."*

– LOUIE'S STORY – THE INTERVIEW

"Dogs were worshipped in Paris
with an adoration envied
by most village priests."

– WAITING IN PARIS

"Cats,
as anyone knows,
are proud creatures and deserve better
from the people who dare to own them."

– A BANK IN PARIS

"She was a tedious little human being,
who thought a cat might actually care what she did
beyond providing him with his creature comforts,
but then again, she was his little human being."

– AN ODD BOUQUET FROM PARIS

"He always was the showman,
the cat who had to have the last word on every subject."

– UNDER A PARIS SKY

"She didn't need much.
A good book.
An amicable cat."
– AN ODD BOUQUET FROM PARIS

"French men,
as well as their cats,
teased."
– AN ODD BOUQUET FROM PARIS

"As a cat,
he's a far better human being than most husbands.
At least, I know where he sleeps after midnight."

– UNDER A PARIS SKY

"She made no attempt to retrieve him, or scold him,
having given up any hope of the furry old bachelor
becoming a permanent house cat.
Some males were simply born to pursue romance."

- UNDER A PARIS SKY

*"Given the choice of a husband or a cat,
I prefer a cat."*

– AN ODD BOUQUET FROM PARIS

*"(He) spent the rest of the day in her lap.
Sometimes a cat had to do – what a cat had to do.
After all, she was the one with the paws
that could operate a can opener
and the latch on the window."*

– UNDER A PARIS SKY

"It was good to be a Parisian cat with perfect eyesight and an even more perfect nose for solving mysteries."

– UNDER A PARIS SKY

"There were as many cat burglars in Paris as there were cats. "

– OUT OF TIME IN PARIS

*"I might never have suspected that the poodle
was aiding and abetting an art thief."*

– FOUND AND LOST IN PARIS

*"He'd diaper her dog's butt
and take the pooch to mass,
if only she'd make him part of her household."*

– OUT OF TIME IN PARIS

*"For six weeks,
he planned to live like a friendly dog without a home."*

– OUT OF TIME IN PARIS

*"With several large parks,
providing a host of squirrels to chase
and an occasional cat to lick,
life here is quite satisfying for man and beast."*

– FOUND AND LOST IN PARIS

"When a person goes home to a cat,
it is easy to forget some people have a wife waiting."

– AN ODD BOUQUET FROM PARIS

"There were times and places
that a cat needed to remind his owner
– who was boss and who was pet.
Tonight was that time
and under this Paris sky was the place."

– UNDER A PARIS SKY

"Truly. What more does a man need?
Oui, you are quite right –
a faithful companion."

– FOUND AND LOST IN PARIS

"I love my dog,
despite his political views."

– AN ODD BOUQUET FROM PARIS

*"When was love ever a practical pursuit
and romance not worth the chase?"*

– OUT OF TIME IN PARIS

*"He had accepted long ago,
regardless of what had been forged on his entry credentials,
he was an alley cat
and alley cats did not pretend."*

- A KEY TO PARIS

"Caesar was a French cat.
He deserved French prayers."

-UNDERGROUND, L' autre Métro

"Melancholy follows me through Paris
like a pair of four-legged shadows,
loyal, devoted, and barking at my heels to be fed."

– WAITING IN PARIS

*"He was to her surprise, quite different
from the other men brought home like abandoned cats.
This one, was more of a pedigreed puppy, a fallen star,
a disrobed Royal who was learning to live as a peasant...
abandoned in France through no fault of his own."*

-A BANK IN PARIS

Les Codes Français
The French Rules

"To him,
*Paris would always be **La Vie en Rose***
and everyone in it, of noble heart."

– UNDERGROUND, L' autre Métro

🏁🏁🏁

*"The French know the intrinsic value
of holding on to the past,
its pleasures, its promises, and its tender mercies."*

- THE PROMISE, Ypóschesi

*"Paris was a place
where anyone could belong."*

– LATE PASSENGER

🏁🏁🏁

*"Once a person had obtained French citizenship,
it no longer mattered where he was born
and it was rude to ask."*

– A BANK IN PARIS

*"In Paris,
everything could be fixed for a price,
even a man's place in history."*

– A LETTER FROM PARIS

"I have been accused of many things in my life...
Gigolo, of course!
Politician?
Never!"

"French law
guaranteed French citizens the right to be
both insulted and assaulted in their native language."

"I did not know why
he had been chosen to be a warrior, and I, a caretaker.
However, we were both now joined to one noble cause,
to protect a fair maiden"

"This was Paris...
People here did not surrender
to artificial rules and regulations.
They tolerated, ignored, or cursed them,
but they never surrendered to them.

🚩🚩🚩

"...a man,
even one who may be dead,
must respect a nation of laws.
After all, France made him famous."

\- FOUND AND LOST IN PARIS

🚩🚩🚩

L' Amour Toujours, Français
Love & La Femme Fatale

"He was indiscreet,
even by Parisian standards."

– THE SEASONS IN THE GARDEN

*"She had lived on the streets of Paris too long,
not to trust her instincts."*

– THE MIST OF MONTMARTRE

*"The men of Paris
did not seem to care that she was ordinary,
only that she was available."*

– THE MIST OF MONTMARTRE

♥

"She came to Paris and changed our lives forever."

- THE SEASONS IN THE GARDEN

"She was in her ignorance
... dangerous."

– THE CLUE, L' Indice

♥

♥

"Hadn't she learned anything
by living in Paris?"

– PARIS APARTMENT FOR RENT

"Paris was a city
full of unfinished love letters."

- A LETTER FROM PARIS

♥

♥

*"She had come to Paris
wanting so much to be remembered,
to be immortalized,
to be loved by strangers
for centuries after her death..."*

– THE MIST OF MONTMARTRE

*"He had learned Lesson One.
Let French women tell you what they want."*

– PARIS APARTMENT FOR RENT

♥

♥

"Paris,
like love,
may not fix us.
But it can make us forget ...
we were ever broken."
– A KEY TO PARIS

"As all Parisians knew,
a woman was not considered interesting,
until she had a past worth hiding."
– A KEY TO PARIS

♥

♥

*"In Paris,
one could assume quite safely,
there were always at least two people
involved in any marriage,
and rarely less than three."*

\- A LETTER FROM PARIS

*"Hemingway was correct.
Paris was a moveable feast
and romance was always on the menu."*

\- A LETTER FROM PARIS

♥

♥

"He said
between Heaven and Earth,
there is this magical place called Paris
and I believed him..."

- The Education of Francine Robinsworth Duchesney

A SUMMER ABROAD

"To be a single woman in Paris
is only asking for trouble
or for a very full dance card."

- FRANCESCA'S STORY – THE INTERVIEW

♥

♥

"Always, better friends than lovers,
we turned our late night bedroom conversations
into gripping confessions,
trading truths for lies"

– THE CLUE, L'Indice

"She had fallen in love.
If not with me,
then, with Paris."

- LOUIE'S STORY – THE INTERVIEW

♥

♥

*"She saw Paris for the first time
as a reflection in her lover's eyes."*

- A BANK IN PARIS

*"In Paris,
for a young woman alone,
there were many ways to learn a new language.
Dancing the tango in the park with strangers
was only one of many."*

– A KEY TO PARIS

♥

"This was Paris.
How could she deny herself
the chance to fall in love?"

- The Education of Francine Robinsworth Duchesney

A SUMMER ABROAD

"A fling in Paris
in the summer?
Well, of course!"

- LOUIE'S STORY – THE INTERVIEW

♥

*"This is the magic of Paris.
What might happen is always a question."*

– AN ODD BOUQUET FROM PARIS

*"It had never occurred to her,
in Paris,
she was the other woman."*

- AN ODD BOUQUET FROM PARIS

♥

♥

*"When I was young
I did what all young men do in Paris.
Once or twice.*

I searched for love."

*Lesson Four:
Proper French women
allow male visitors to knock twice.*

– PARIS APARTMENT FOR RENT

♥

♥

"Lesson Eight:
Some women
don't wait for two knocks at the door."

– PARIS APARTMENT FOR RENT

"He came to Paris
to be liberated from the darkness of his destiny
only to discover in the City of Light –
a man can never escape his passion."

– A BANK IN PARIS

♥

♥

"She would never understand, as long as she lived,
how people could enjoy the dance,
when they refused to learn the steps."

\- A KEY TO PARIS

"This was Paris.
Age had nothing to do with a person's chance
for finding love or romance
or the prospect of creating a scandal."

\- A KEY TO PARIS

♥

♥

*"Lesson Nine:
Sincere flattery is more valuable than
... truffles."*
– PARIS APARTMENT FOR RENT

*"Love demanded a generous heart,
not necessarily a generous purse.
They often stole other men's wives or other wives' husbands.
It was refreshingly French."*
- A LETTER FROM PARIS

♥

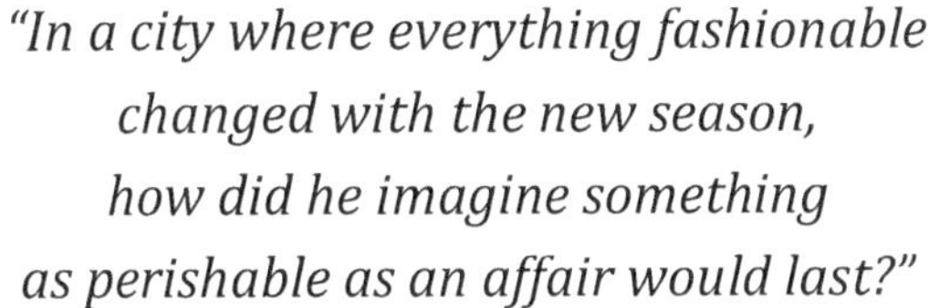

*"In a city where everything fashionable
changed with the new season,
how did he imagine something
as perishable as an affair would last?"*

– A BANK IN PARIS

*"She murmured the only truth she knew.
I miss Paris."*

- FOUND AND LOST IN PARIS

♥

*"Each of these men did love,
as best as any devotee of careless romance can."*

- FOUND AND LOST IN PARIS

*"In one of life's greatest ironies,
a man's past follows him
like the shadow of an abandoned lover."*

-A BANK IN PARIS

♥

La Haute Couture Française
The French look

"Hypocrisy,
a global child,
embraced no nationality
or wore any exclusive monogram."

-AN ODD BOUQUET FROM PARIS

"It seemed she was the only person in all of Paris without an umbrella."

– THE MIST OF MONTMARTRE

"Everyone in Paris has a price.
Everyone is selling something.
Some of us are simply more honest about it."

– THE MIST OF MONTMARTRE

*"The River Seine divided many things in Paris:
lifestyles, politics, incomes, fashions,
desires..."*

*"If he was going to live in Paris,
he needed to look Parisian."*

"You try so hard to be Parisian,
but I can see you wear your heart outside your shirt."

- PARIS APARTMENT FOR RENT

"Paris in the rain was a perfect place
for displaying a broken heart."

– A KEY TO PARIS

❦ ❦ ❦

*"There were originals and there were imposters.
In Paris,
a person knew which one he or she was."*

- A LETTER FROM PARIS

*"She traveled in fashion circles,
not literary ones."*

– THE PROMISE, Ypōschesi

֍ ֍ ֍

*"Each week,
new perfumes announced the arrival
of new strangers to entice and entertain."*

– THE SEASONS IN THE GARDEN

*"Her fashion was suited for the boudoir,
not a café,
but she did not care.*

– THE SEASONS IN THE GARDEN

֍ ֍ ֍

ℛℛℛ

"Young women of a now lost society,
contemporaries who enviously had mimicked her style,
had no idea what secrets lay beneath
the silk and satin camouflage. "

– A BANK IN PARIS

"In this fashion capitol,
it was not so very unusual to see people drinking champagne
at 8:00 o'clock in the morning,
looking as if they had just departed a masquerade ball."

– A BANK IN PARIS

ℛℛℛ

*"A great many fashion faux pas
could be hidden beneath a raincoat,
even a sad-looking crumpled one."*

- A KEY TO PARIS

*"'If her fashion sense was any indication
of her cooperative nature,
changing her embrace of celibacy
was going to be a difficult task for any man."*

- A KEY TO PARIS

*"Regardless of their stations in life,
people in Paris wanted to look stylish and appear as rich
as the people they served."*

– LATE PASSENGERS

*"...The ever more prevalent scarf,
an essential fashion statement that determined
if they were French or only pretending to be."*

- LATE PASSENGER

*"Where Coco strolled,
the world followed."*

– LATE PASSENGER

*"Has anyone seen my purse?" She asks.
"I never know if she wants us to admire
her latest fashion accessory,
or to find where she left it."*

- THE SEASONS IN THE GARDEN

"Fashion was all about the new season."

*"I don't trust your heart
any more than I trust your fashion sense."*

꧁꧂

*"You understand that some people come to Paris
with the precise intention of becoming lost.
The city does encourage that sort of luxury."*

- FOUND AND LOST IN PARIS

Les Mangeurs de Gâteaux Français

The French Cake Eaters

"*Paris
was a city decorated with rich women.*"

– A KEY TO PARIS

"*The rich muddled through,
lost in a well-orchestrated ebb and flow of dinner invitations,
never knowing one moment of hunger,
unless they were dieting.*"

– THE MIST OF MONTMARTRE

"He knew people
by the jewels they owned
or needed to sell..."

– TOO RICH FOR RAIN

"In those days,
the rich enjoyed the upper stories
because the streets below were filled with poor people.
They preferred to freeze to death in eagle nests,
rather than sweat with the peasants in pigeonholes."

- A BANK IN PARIS

*"The rich didn't need to rise before noon.
They had people who would."*

– TOO RICH FOR RAIN

*"Marriage to a rich, older man
had turned the girl into a woman,
and the woman into a stranger."*

- THE CLUE, L'Indice

*"Money was power.
Money bought freedom."*

– TOO RICH FOR RAIN

*"Money had become proof of love
for other people,
but not for me."*

- THE CLUE, L'Indice

They gravitated to the Mediterranean
for the same reasons everyone else did.
The weather. The water. The food.
The anonymity.

- GAMAN

"It was not his fault that he was trapped in the upper classes
or that he had been born rich.
It was an inherited burden."

– THE MIST OF MONTMARTRE

*"Parisians always suspect the rich
of hiding something."*

– A BANK IN PARIS

*"Being rich or royal
did not guarantee a pure heart
or an innocent character."*

– A BANK IN PARIS

*"A man was challenged every day to ignore the poverty
that lay beneath the wealth
dripping from Haussmann balconies."*

– WAITING IN PARIS

*"The rich need the poor
as much as the poor do the rich."*

– OUT OF TIME IN PARIS

*"Some of the richest people she had met in Paris
were among the most notorious."*

– AN ODD BOUQUET FROM PARIS

*"This was 21st Century Paris and in this era,
the rich and poor negotiated the price of tolerance
on street corners."*

– WAITING IN PARIS

*"The richest layer of this supposedly classless society
represented nearly all of my potential clients."*

– WAITING IN PARIS

*"If someone had to explain
what he did for a living,
he was probably too poor to be here."*

- TOO RICH FOR RAIN

Les Poches Vides

Empty Pockets

" In Rome,
he might have died rich quickly or died poor slowly,
but either way he would have died.
Forced to live in exile in Paris,
(he) was at the very least alive."

-AN ODD BOUQUET IN PARIS

*"For a poor college backpacker,
who had never seen anything of the world
before that summer trip to Europe,
it was love at first sight."*

- THE CLUE, L' Indice

*"I was not rich,
but I was American.
She was too young to understand the difference."*

- THE CLUE, L' Indice

&&& &&& &&&

"Among the working poor of Paris,
silence could be secured for a price – especially,
if it came with promises of limitless future purchases."

– THE MIST OF MONTMARTRE

"There was a charm about him
that could have made a poor man rich."

– THE MIST OF MONTMARTRE

*"The poor of Paris are not without
their own interesting friends."*

– A BANK IN PARIS

*"While the poor did not know the troubles of abundance,
the rich were denied the hidden rewards of poverty,
a loaf of bread shared."*

– THE MIST OF MONTMARTRE

🏃🏃🏃

"Give me a poor man
who has no hope of becoming rich
and I will show you an honest man."

– OUT OF TIME IN PARIS

"Poor people were content to view great art in museums.
They did not need it
hanging on the walls of their fifth floor walkup."

– WAITING IN PARIS

75

*"Poets die poor
and their wives... poorer."*

*"A poor man would have rotted in jail all these years,
but not a rich one."*

*"The poor negotiated leases on closet-sized apartments
with as much acumen as one might spend
on choosing his final resting place on Earth,
knowing that a long line waited for one to die,
so that another could move in."*

– THE MIST OF MONTMARTRE

*"So, again...
I buy dinner.
Your heart is making me a poor man."*

– FOUND AND LOST IN PARIS

"I had done the unforgiveable
by breaking her heart,
by admitting the truth
... that I was poor."

– THE PROMISE, Ypōschesi

L' Aristocrate Français
The French Waiter

"He was born to be a waiter in Paris.
We should all be so lucky
to know our place in the universe."

– AN ODD BOUQUET FROM PARIS

*"Waiters in Paris knew everyone
and therefore,
everything worth knowing."*

– WAITING IN PARIS

*"Their rude visitor did not wait to be acknowledged,
choosing instead to lift his fingers and snap
in that red flag way that excited the blood
of every waiter in Paris."*

– UNDER A PARIS SKY

*"A waiter was as much an enforcer of the laws of civility
as was the police detective
who seemed intent upon violating them."*

– UNDER A PARIS SKY

*"The waiter was not being rude.
He simply did not feel compelled
to show the extent of his dentist's talents
every time he delivered a glass of wine or a basket of bread."*

– A BANK IN PARIS

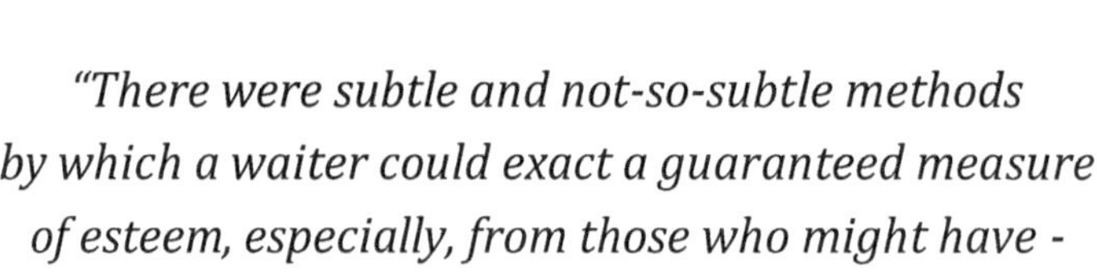

"He's not a poet.
He's a waiter."

– WAITING IN PARIS

"There were subtle and not-so-subtle methods
by which a waiter could exact a guaranteed measure
of esteem, especially, from those who might have -
egregiously - forgotten to pay tribute."

– WAITING IN PARIS

*"Waiters belonged to a private club with secretive rules
and possibly, even a secret handshake
or kiss on the cheek."*

– WAITING IN PARIS

*"In every way that seemed to matter in France,
he was also a very handsome man
and the quintessential French waiter,
mustache et tous!"*

– WAITING IN PARIS

Y 🍽 Y

*"If tourists want to be served by friendly waiters
who show their teeth,
they should stay in America."*

– WAITING IN PARIS

*"Their second offensive act
was to commandeer one of the choicest tables,
and their third, committed by rearranging the chairs.
These, as all Parisian waiters know,
were declarations of war."*

- A KEY TO PARIS

Y 🍽 Y

*"There are many waiters in Paris,
but very few billionaires with generous appetites."*
– WAITING IN PARIS

*"How much a waiter remembered
and how much was forgotten
made for interesting investigations.
I could question waiters all day and all night long
with a glass in one hand and a fork in the other."*
- WAITING IN PARIS

*"Fast food in Paris
was not really that fast."*

– NEVER CHANGE, Montmartre

*"Bread that can last a month?
Incroyable!"*

- A KEY TO PARIS

Le Royauté Français
The French Chef

"Restaurants in Paris were like mistresses.
If a man visited a favorite only once a week,
he had to make the chef believe
he starved the other six days."

– WAITING IN PARIS

"(His) education in wine making began
on the day he was born
and at the winery where his mother gave birth,
making him a self-proclaimed wine expert."

\- THE SEASONS IN THE GARDEN

"I can't help the way I look. Angry chef, (He) said,
running a finger down the center of his scar.
"I should have ducked."

\- PARIS APARTMENT FOR RENT

"The chef?
I have no idea where he is.
Have you looked in the wine cellar?
(Or your wife's bed?)"

– FOUND AND LOST IN PARIS

"People learned what satisfied their appetites and then,
built their lives around those who fed those cravings.
(He) was, at least in his youth, always on someone's menu."

- A JAZZ CLUB IN PARIS

*"Crowds gathered around them, to read today's specialties
and discuss this Chef and that Chef –
as if they were movie stars."*

– LOUIE'S STORY – THE INTERVIEW

*"For him, a man ending jazz club haunts at dawn,
one o'clock in the afternoon
was a perfectly suitable time for eggs."*

– A BANK IN PARIS

*"With a quick hand,
a sudden sprinkle of red pepper on his waiting bowls of soup,
a chef could bring a man to his knees."*

– WAITING IN PARIS

*"You will make the chef smile, if you order the trout.
You will make your stomach smile, if you don't."*

– WAITING IN PARIS

*"Regardless of how safe one thinks he is,
he would do well to know where he is
on someone else's food chain."*

– FOUND AND LOST IN PARIS

*"Peasant and aristocrat
are not nearly so defined by wealth
as they are by what's on their plate."*

- WAITING IN PARIS

Le Voisin Français

The French Neighbor

"*In Paris,*
each building was a sort of village."

– PARIS APARTMENT FOR RENT

∞∞∞

∞∞∞

*"I bought the place
because this will be my last home in Paris."*

– NEVER CHANGE, Montmartre

*"A small artist's studio
shared with an insanely talented, but drunken impressionist,
a place where only one man could make love for the night,
was not enough."*

– AN ODD BOUQUET FROM PARIS

∞∞∞

∞∞∞

"*Paris was not so different
from her small home town.*"

"*It was also a very hip neighborhood,
if hip meant walls covered in wild displays of graffiti
and flowers fertilized with dog excrement.*"

– LOUIE'S STORY – THE INTERVIEW

∞∞∞

∞∞∞

96

"A Parisian's home was his castle,
albeit a tiny one."

- A LETTER FROM PARIS

"Some buildings in Paris were run like small villages,
and in matters of a suspicious nature,
the concierge served as the centurion."

– A BANK IN PARIS

∞∞∞

∽∽∽

"Lesson Seven:
Be patient.
Eventually, you will win over the French.
It takes time."

- PARIS APARTMENT FOR RENT

"Most buildings were locked up after 7 p.m.,
when even the concierge went home for dinner."

– A BANK IN PARIS

∽∽∽

∽∽∽

"Someone in Paris
must have left her window open…
again."'

- UNDER A PARIS SKY

"In Paris,
a lack of inhibition was critical to peaceful co-existence."

– AN ODD BOUQUET FROM PARIS

∽∽∽

L'Écrivain Français
The French writer

"*I came to Paris to write.*

*It was Paris's history that drew me here,
but my personal history that made me stay.
I could no longer go home.
My footprints had been erased.*"

THE PROMISE, Ypóschesi

"Without truth,
I was forced to imagine his answers,
but I was a writer. I could do that."

- THE PROMISE, Ypōschesi

"But, an idea painted carefully and gently by an artist,
for instance... an artist of words?
Well... That is the most seductive."

- THE SEASONS IN THE GARDEN

– NEVER CHANGE, Montmartre

– THE SEASONS IN THE GARDEN

*"I've too much to do today
to waste time being insulted by someone
who no longer owns a library card."*

– AN ODD BOUQUET IN PARIS

*"Paris, unlike London, offered a writer more.
It permitted one to become
unembarrassed and uninhibited,
to become a cake eater."*

- THE SEASONS IN THE GARDEN

*"Life was meant to be a mystery
full of unfinished chapters."*

– UNDER A PARIS SKY

*"You are a writer,
but take my advice, my friend.
You should write more, and talk less."*

- THE CLUE, L' Indice

"In Paris,
she had begun writing her own history."

- A LETTER FROM PARIS

"As far as I could tell,
they had accepted my word that I was a writer.
One day, they would need proof."

– THE SEASONS IN THE GARDEN

"I suppose – once a journalist, always a journalist,"
she had mumbled as if it were the lowest form of writer.
"I prefer poets."

– WAITING IN PARIS

"I hoped that, one day, I would no longer be considered
just another lost writer in search of a home."

– OUT OF TIME IN PARIS

"Writing, not cat poop, was the focus of my life in the loft,
although I had met a few editors,
who after reading some of my work,
might have disagreed."

- THE CLUE, L' Indice

L'Artiste Français
The French Artist

"They arrived on his doorstep
in the manner of models seeking celebrity on canvas,
patrons offering to buy a painting in exchange
for closer encounters with the artist, and heirs who,
having grown bored with their last martini,
were seeking new amusement."

-AN ODD BOUQUET FROM PARIS

*"Artist and the man were one in the same
and Paris was his blank canvas."*

*"I had come to Paris as a blank canvas.
I welcomed these artists of social change,
who were eager to paint my future along with theirs."*

*"Le Sacré Coeur.
If I had not already chosen to be a writer,
perhaps, this view alone
would have inspired my becoming an artist."*

– THE UNDERGROUND, L' autre Métro

*"I am an artist,
so I can see below the surface."*

– LOUIE'S STORY – THE INTERVIEW

"Here was a masterpiece no man could have created
and no artist could capture on canvas."

- THE PROMISE, Ypōschesi

"He was a mentor,
an artist,
but with a writer's soul."

- THE PROMISE, Ypōschesi

"Real women needed to be fed, not starved.
Every great artist knew that.
Every great artist painted that."

– A KEY TO PARIS

"An artist's creation,
like an afternoon of romance,
could awaken their senses and bring meaning to life."

– A LETTER FROM PARIS

*"An artist
preventing another artist from working was unthinkable!
Revolutions had begun for lesser reasons!"*

– LOUIE'S STORY – THE INTERVIEW

*"Any young man, calling himself an artist,
could count on being generously received
by older richer women who lived for more
than artistic inspiration."*

– LOUIE'S STORY – THE INTERVIEW

*"If I had not been born an artist,
I would have become a philosopher."*

– AN ODD BOUQUET FROM PARIS

*"(He) had introduced himself as an artist looking for models,
making a point of dressing as though he knew
exactly who or what he was looking for
and could afford to pay for either."*

– AN ODD BOUQUET FROM PARIS

*"(He) had a reputation in the Parisian art world
for collecting women the way other men collected
fine wines and old coins."*

- AN ODD BOUQUET FROM PARIS

*"In death,
I am yet an artist
and my masterpiece is not yet finished."*

- LOST AND FOUND IN PARIS

Le Jazz Français
The French Musician

*"Here, no matter who a man was,
had been, or hoped to become, famous or infamous,
he could let his passions roam freely
and be equally welcomed."*

- A JAZZ CLUB IN PARIS

♫ ♫ ♫

*"His arena was below ground in Paris,
in zigzag tunnels of jazz clubs
and places where government uniforms
were neither wanted nor welcome."*

– A BANK IN PARIS

*"I no longer needed the image
so artistically painted on the bare back of a young jazz singer
to explain his choice of Paris over Rome."*

- LOUIE'S STORY – THE INTERVIEW

♬ ♬ ♬

"Where he lived,
any musician moving in would be treated like a celebrity
and his free entertainment would be welcomed."

– AN ODD BOUQUET FROM PARIS

"Upon returning home late one night,
he was struck on the head by his saxophone
being tossed from a second floor window.

The concierge swore in court that he wasn't the culprit,
suggesting that there was more than one music critic
living in the building."

- AN ODD BOUQUET FROM PARIS

♬ ♬ ♬

"Drawn by two things
– a passion for jazz and a desire for anonymity –
they slipped in through back doors,
nodded silent hellos to bartenders,
and fell half dazed into the darkest corners."

"He returned home from nights in a new jazz club,
as if he were the first man in history to discover music;
the first to smoke a cigar; the first to taste calvados;
... the first to savor the bright red lips
of a salaciously dressed cabaret performer."

♬ ♬ ♬

Le Night Bloomer Français

The dangerously French

*"This man was a
"fiore notte"
(a night bloomer)."*

– A BANK IN PARIS

"In Paris,
anyone willing to give away his time for free,
doesn't have much to sell."

– AN ODD BOUQUET IN PARIS

"Some of the sleepers were prey,
some of them, predators.
Some of them, like her, were angels who worked tirelessly
to tether spirits to the Earth for one more day. "

- THE SEASONS IN THE GARDEN

*"There were those who only haunted Paris in the dark.
They were the night bloomers."*

- OUT OF TIME IN PARIS

*"He loved the coolness of dark narrow cobblestone streets
and shadowy underground jazz clubs,
where he fit in easily among the other night bloomers."*

– UNDER A PARIS SKY

*"Darkness could hide a great many sins
as well as a sinner's age."*

-UNDER A PARIS SKY

*"Over the years,
he had become more comfortable
beneath the streets of Paris, than he was above."*

-AN ODD BOUQUET FROM PARIS

Le Jardin Français
The French Garden

"For a woman who had grown up on a farm,
she was woefully lacking the skills required
of any woman hoping to catch a farmer's attention.
However, she was very good at attracting cats."

- AN ODD BOUQUET FROM PARIS

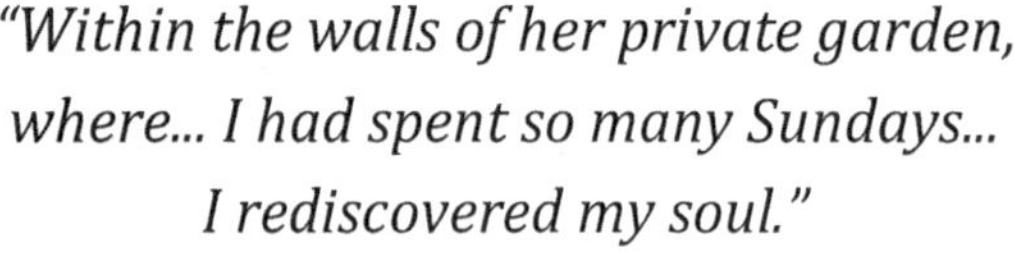

"...the size of the garden does not matter,
only the passion of the gardener."

- THE SEASONS IN THE GARDEN

"Within the walls of her private garden,
where... I had spent so many Sundays...
I rediscovered my soul."

- UNDERGROUND, L' autre Métro

*"Life gives us, by endless examples,
opportunities to grow, to adapt, and to change.
Gardeners understand this."*

- THE SEASONS IN THE GARDEN

*"Perhaps,
to others in Paris,
I was a weed in their garden."*

- THE SEASONS IN THE GARDEN

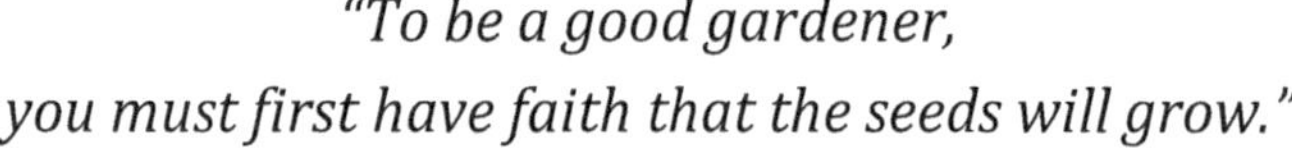

*"I attribute her serenity
to the fact that she gardens."*

- THE SEASONS IN THE GARDEN

*"To be a good gardener,
you must first have faith that the seeds will grow."*

- THE SEASONS IN THE GARDEN

"Night Bloomers.
Ideal for gardeners, who cannot sleep."

- THE SEASONS IN THE GARDEN

"The growing season, just like her life,
had a rhythm, a pattern.
It was one, which she could not change."

- THE CLUE, L'Indice

"In France,
even flowerpots had to be fashionably updated
each new season."

– AN ODD BOUQUET FROM PARIS

Les Grandes Vacances Françaises
The Grand Escape

*"I don't need liquor.
I need a holiday!"*

– OUT OF TIME IN PARIS

"Deaths, like births, were expected.
Changing one's holiday?
Never!"

– UNDERGROUND, L' autre Métro

"Leisure is a rich man's folly."

– OUT OF TIME IN PARIS

"There were weekends
and summer holidays in San Tropez,
but those – he considered necessities."

– A BANK IN PARIS

"You think les Grandes Vacances serve no good purpose,
but without a holiday,
a man is totally worthless."

– OUT OF TIME IN PARIS

*"Simply to sit among friends in an outside café
was a holiday for me. "*

– OUT OF TIME IN PARIS

*"They found me in a bar after one of their days at sea.
The details of how we connected remain blurry,
but one of them must have found me amusing in that way
that people from L.A. find people from New York amusing,
as if Manhattan were a foreign country."*

-THE PROMISE, Ypóschesi

"Summer,
like a Toulouse-painted lady in a bright red hat,
had marched in, sat down,
and refused to leave until paid."

"Hotel clerks had a nasty habit of recording
who came and who went,
especially when guests looked familiar
and were worth remembering."

△ △ △

*"She was not the sort of woman
who would hide a lover somewhere in the south of France
and then, tell her partner that she was off to Africa
on holiday."*

- UNDER A PARIS SKY

*"She was a sucker for good-looking, smooth-talking,
dangerous men from the south of France.
In that, there was another story to tell,
but at another time."*

- PARIS APARTMENT FOR RENT

Le Malaise Français

To suffer... not so quietly

"*Her melancholy*
was an incurable plague in Paris."

- AN ODD BOUQUET FROM PARIS

*"He came to Paris to be liberated
from the darkness of his destiny..."*

- A BANK IN PARIS

*"Living in Denial must be like bathing in olive oil.
Reality never penetrates deeply enough
to give one an apparent rash."*

- FOUND AND LOST IN PARIS

"Lesson Three:
Don't enter a pharmacy unless your life depends upon it. ...
His allergy paled in comparison
to the guy with the Black Plague on aisle three."

– PARIS APARTMENT FOR RENT

"Not all artists suffer
the loss of an ear, a heart, a soul...
but nonetheless, they must suffer."

– FOUND AND LOST IN PARIS

*"Only when death knocked on his door
did he dare consider himself in need
of authentic companionship."*

– FOUND AND LOST IN PARIS

*"His were the words
that she had waded through 17 years of misery
and a hundred romance novels to hear.
How could she deny him anything?"*

- FRANCESCA'S STORY – THE INTERVIEW

Au Revoir,
Mes Amis Français
To Die French

*"Death,
like most events in life,
looked uncomplicated on paper."*

\- AN ODD BOUQUET FROM PARIS

*"Your passions, Mon Ami,
will have half of Paris dancing on your grave...
but they will be dancing the tango."*

- AN ODD BOUQUET FROM PARIS

*"In Paris, he would surrender to either
dying in poverty or becoming a rich woman's toy.
In Leuven, (his friend) would insist the word was gigolo."*

- FRANCESCA'S STORY – THE INTERVIEW

"Serendipity
is an angel in the shadows."

"To live in the moment,
a hero must first surrender his past to his enemies
and his future to the angels."

*"The real cause of death
had been the expense of the wedding."*

– UNDERGROUND, L' autre Métro

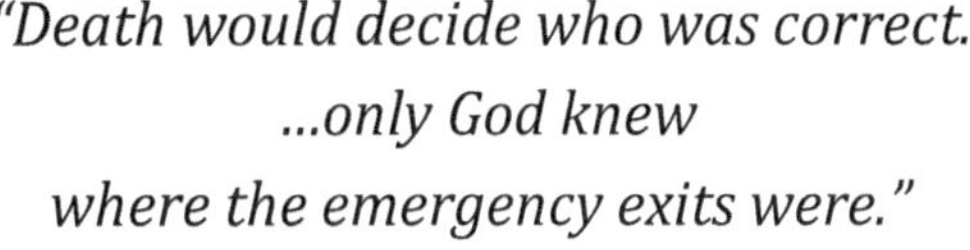

*"Death would decide who was correct.
...only God knew
where the emergency exits were."*

– NEVER CHANGE, Montmartre

*"For to be without her
was death itself."*

– A BANK IN PARIS

*"Only in death
are most of us remembered as masters of our craft
and usually, by those who do not have appreciation
for the cost of an artist's life."*

– FOUND AND LOST IN PARIS

*"When a man stares death in the face,
he can become very motivated
and very inventive."*

– LOUIE'S STORY – THE INTERVIEW

*"Thus is the expectation of starving artists,
whose stories bring them nearer to accolades of sheer genius
in deathly repose,
rather than while still breathing their regrets
of unrequited love."*

– FOUND AND LOST IN PARIS

*"(He) had become too cherished a friend,
to allow something as transient as death
to separate them."*

-A LETTER FROM PARIS

*"In France, you would die,
if you could not eat onions."*

- PARIS APARTMENT FOR RENT

*"In death, I am yet an artist
and my masterpiece is not yet finished."*

- FOUND AND LOST IN PARIS

Best Regards,
PARIS

*"Entre ciel et terre,
il ya Paris."*

*"Between Heaven and Earth,
there is Paris."*

– A KEY TO PARIS

"Paris was about souls,
not sidewalks."

- THE PROMISE, Ypōschesi

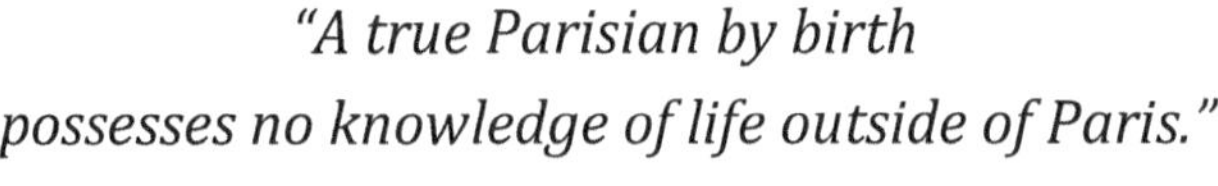

"A true Parisian by birth
possesses no knowledge of life outside of Paris."

- THE SEASONS IN THE GARDEN

"This is Paris.
Here, a person is never alone."

- WAITING IN PARIS

"My appetite for Paris
was whetted once before in my youth,
and I had been wholly seduced.
A warm spring night requires no imagination."

- THE SEASONS IN THE GARDEN

"A new map for my life is being charted here in Paris."

- THE SEASONS IN THE GARDEN

"Who planned to sleep anyway?
This was Paris."

– NEVER CHANGE, Montmartre

*"It was a familiar world
filled with jazz musicians, poets, writers, artists,
and more importantly for his refined pleasures –
impetuous companions who did not own watches."*

– AN ODD BOUQUET FROM PARIS

"I had come to Paris as a blank canvas."

- THE SEASONS IN THE GARDEN

"Paris
had shown her in some parts of the world
women could flaunt their emotions,
and still be welcomed into society."

– GAMAN

"This was Paris,
where all things were possible,
and nothing was ever, quite, as it appeared to be."

– A KEY TO PARIS

*"Paris
was a place big enough to hide
one more stranger."*

- THE SEASONS IN THE GARDEN

*"If there was anything wrong with the world,
the people in Paris seemed unaware of it."*

– A KEY TO PARIS

*"How could he trust someone
with the most intimate details of his life,
if that person did not love Paris?"*

- GAMAN

*"You understand that some people come to Paris
with the precise intention of becoming lost.
The city does encourage that sort of luxury."*

- FOUND AND LOST IN PARIS

"She could only envision her life in Paris."

- UNDERGROUND, L' autre Métro

"On Sundays in Paris,
for most people,
the world stopped turning."

- A KEY TO PARIS

*"The City of Light was a magical place for anyone
with an open mind,
a warm heart,
and a hidden past."*

- A LETTER FROM PARIS

*"In Paris,
he felt quite abandoned by time."*

- LOUIE'S STORY – THE INTERVIEW

"After being in Paris only a short time,
I was beginning to believe
almost anything was possible here."

- FRANCESCA'S STORY – THE INTERVIEW

"In Paris,
as a young man free to live his life
without the weighty burden of the puritanical guilt
I had carried for 20 years of my existence,
I was confused."

- WAITING IN PARIS

"He believed that in Paris
it did not take long for anyone's destiny
or desire to become known."

- UNDER A PARIS SKY

"Enlightenment was crucial
to the survival of all Parisians."

- THE SEASONS IN THE GARDEN

"I would return to Paris,
specifically to Montmartre.
This was where I was meant to live, love, and die."

– NEVER CHANGE, Montmartre

"She had always found excuses
not to leave Paris."

- A LETTER FROM PARIS

"It was comforting to know that Paris would be here,
long after I was no longer walking its streets
or the earth."

- THE PROMISE, Ypōschesi

Le Justice Français
Winged Victory

I keep Paris forever.

I win."

- FRANCESCA'S STORY – THE INTERVIEW

Merci for your purchase!

If you would like to recommend this book,
or other titles by this author,
S'il vous plaît,

post a review at:
Amazon.com
Goodreads.com

Author photograph © Michael D. Owens

About the Author

Peggy Kopman-Owens has lived and worked in 35 countries on five continents during her career in aviation and as a free-lance writer. While her literary properties include books, screenplays, and stage plays, creating three series of Paris mysteries has become her newest passion.

Presently, there are 27 books by this author available for purchase in print edition, eBook, or audio book. For more information, please visit:

https://www.amazon.com/Peggy-Kopman-Owens/e/B009QPXCUU

Cover Art © Roger Kopman
Online Gallery:
www.KOPMANPHOTOS.com

www.ingramcontent.com/pod-product-compliance
Lightning Source LLC
Chambersburg PA
CBHW070804240726
48654CB00007B/198